GUITAR TUTOR

by
Charles Gregory

Edition **SCHOTT** 10979

FOREWORD

This guitar tutor is not a complete guide to becoming a virtuoso guitar player. It simply shows the beginner the right principles of a technique which will give more satisfaction and fewer disappointments later on if and when starting to study with a teacher.

The disadvantage of a tutor is that it obviously cannot criticize the student as a teacher would. Therefore it is most important to be constantly critical of the basic points of holding and playing the guitar. Unless this is accomplished from the very beginning, great difficulties will arise which can take a long time to rectify.

It is my hope that this guitar tutor, especially with its illustrations, can help the beginner who is not able to have lessons.

CHARLES GREGORY.

CONTENTS

THE GUITAR

It is better for the guitar to have nylon strings because they give a more gentle sound and are far easier to play especially with the left hand.

In the middle the gap should be about one eighth to a qu

At the top of the guitar the open strings should be as near as possible to the metal frets, but they must not rattle when played.

The metal machines at the top of the guitar are used for tuning the strings and should move with very little effort.

of an inch.   THESE POINTS SHOULD BE CHECKED BY A TEACHER OR PLAYER.

YOUR EQUIPMENT

A foot stool four to six inches high for your left foot.

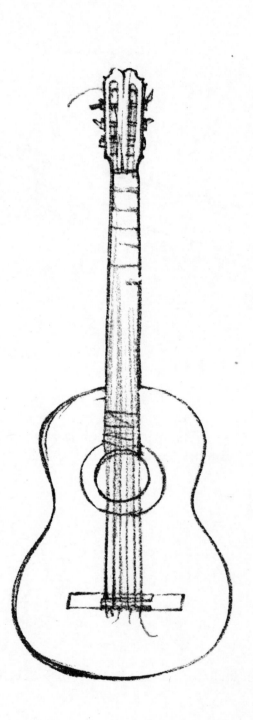

A chair of normal height without armrests.

A nylon strung guitar.

HOW TO HOLD THE GUITAR

1. Left foot on the foot stool.

2. Guitar on your left knee.

3. Right arm round the guitar with the elbow on it.

Fig. 1

4. The guitar must always be kept up-right as in Fig. 1 NOT as in Fig. 2.

Fig. 2

HOW TO TUNE YOUR GUITAR

Tune the top string of the guitar to either ::

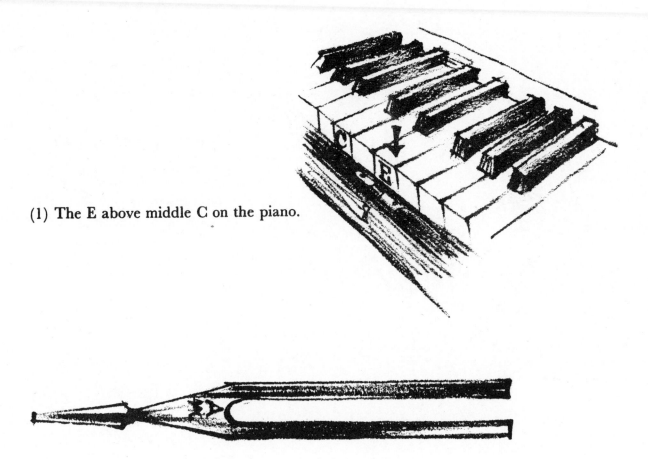

(1) The E above middle C on the piano.

(2) A tuning fork. (Ask for a tuning fork with the pitch of A440). Put the 1st finger on the 5th fret 1st string, this will give the same sound as the tuning fork.

(3) A set of pitch pipes which are especially made for the guitar and have six notes, one for each string.

Having tuned the top (E) string:

Put your 1st finger on the 5th fret, 2nd string, and bring the two strings to the same pitch.
Always alter the lower of the two strings.

Put your 1st finger on the 4th fret, 3rd string,   ,,   ,,   ,,   ,,   ,,

Put your 1st finger on the 5th fret, 4th string,   ,,   ,,   ,,   ,,   ,,

Put your 1st finger on the 5th fret, 5th string,   ,,   ,,   ,,   ,,   ,,

Put your 1st finger on the 5th fret, 6th string,   ,,   ,,   ,,   ,,   ,,

THE FIRST NOTE

Before you begin to play see that your right hand wrist is in the correct position.

The thumb can rest on the bottom string to help keep the wrist in its place. Only do this for the first few times of practice, then take the thumb away as this must not become a habit.

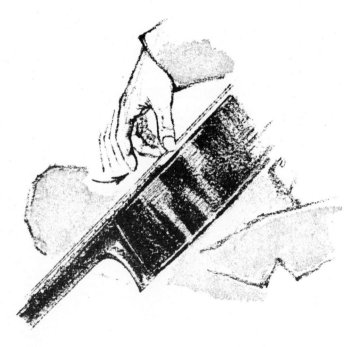

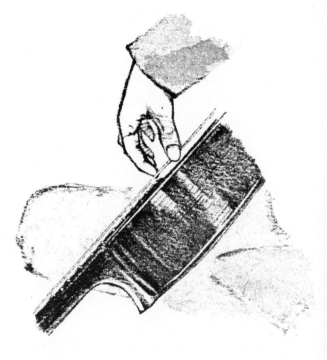

Fig. 1 shows the first right hand finger moving towards the first string.

Fig. 2 shows the first right hand finger striking the first string.

Fig. 3 The 1st finger has played the 1st string and has come to rest on the 2nd string.

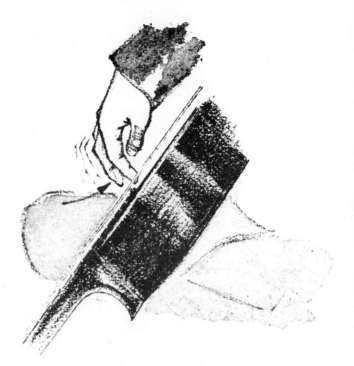

Fig. 4 The 2nd finger now moves towards the 1st string: keep the 1st finger resting against the 2nd string.

Fig. 5 The 2nd finger is hitting the 1st string and the 1st finger is leaving the 2nd string.

Fig. 6 The 2nd finger is now resting against the 2nd string and the 1st finger is ready to play again.

MUSIC AND THE RIGHT HAND

The right hand has special letters to represent each finger:

Thumb = p   1st finger = i   2nd finger = m   3rd finger = a

Play four times on the top string, using 1st and 2nd fingers alternately.

This is how it is written in musical notation.

Play four times on each string except the bass 6th. E B G D A.

     Try not to alter the position of the wrist when playing from one string to another. Move only from the elbow joint.

Two easy studies using the open strings.

Study 1.

Study 2.

LEFT HAND

Try to keep in mind these three points.

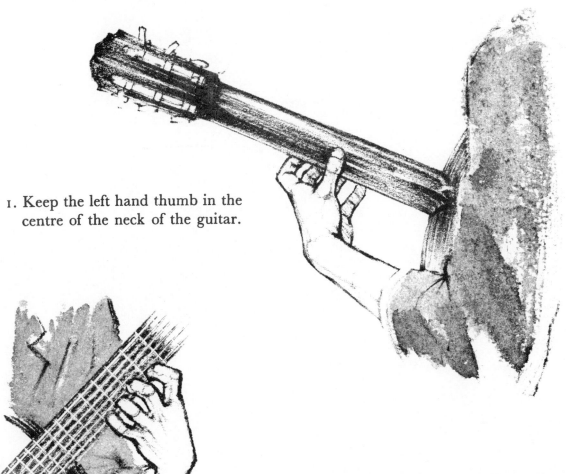

1. Keep the left hand thumb in the centre of the neck of the guitar.

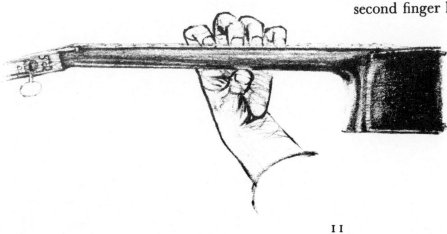

2. Keep the left hand fingers upright all the time.

3. Keep the left hand thumb opposite the second finger left hand.

Always make sure that your left and right hands are in their correct positions before you start.

Each note on the five lines and in the four spaces has a letter name.

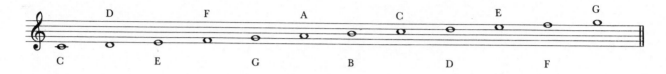

The numbers below indicate the left hand finger as well as the fret which you should use.

Study 3.

These numbers in the circles indicate which string the note is on.
Right hand plays i,m,i,m, all through the piece.

Study 4.

After the Treble clef 𝄞 the figure four over the crotchet means there are four crotchet beats to every bar in the piece.

Study 5.

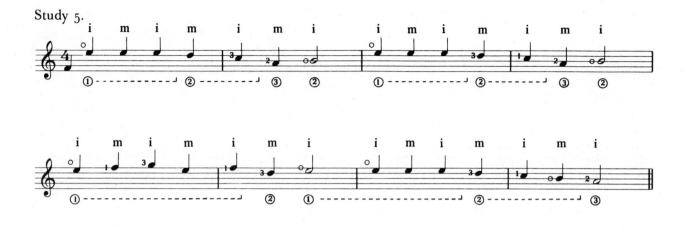

The minim ♩ lasts the length of two crotchets ♩ + ♩ = ♩ .

Study 6.

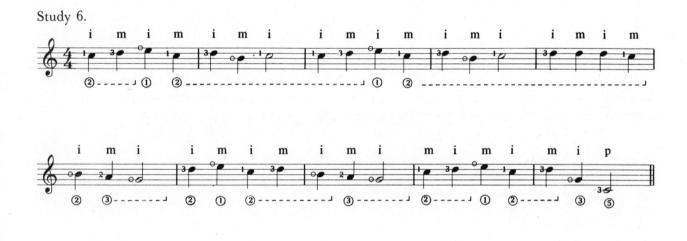

    Notice the crotchet under the four in the time signature has been replaced by a figure 4. So that will now appear as $\frac{4}{4}$, $\frac{2}{4}$ as $\frac{2}{4}$, $\frac{3}{4}$ as $\frac{3}{4}$.

    Also the minim will be replaced in the time signature by the figure 2, so that $\frac{2}{2}$ will now appear as $\frac{2}{2}$. This is because a minim is half a semibreve, and a crotchet is a quarter of a semibreve. Similarly one quaver is an eighth of a semibreve and will now on be replaced by the figure 8, so $\frac{3}{8}$ will now be $\frac{3}{8}$ and $\frac{6}{8}$ will be $\frac{6}{8}$.

Bobby Shaftoe

After the treble clef the sharp sign placed on the top line (F sharp) indicates that all notes of this name throughout the piece must be raised by one fret or semitone. This sign placed before the time signature is called the key signature. In this piece the key is G; and the melody ends on G. If the sharp sign is placed before any note during a piece, it raises that particular note by one fret or semitone and its power lasts for all notes of that name within the bar in which it occurs.

Study 7.

In the second line, second bar, last note the fingering is different. The low note which is G would normally be played with the 3rd finger on the 3rd fret, 6th string but here the note is played with the 2nd finger on the 3rd fret, 6th string.

Yankee Doodle

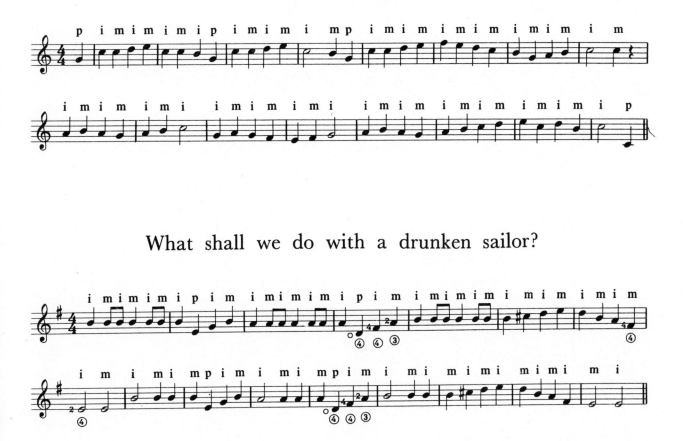

What shall we do with a drunken sailor?

When two notes are played in the duration of one crotchet they are called QUAVERS and are written like this ♪♪ or ♫, ♪♪ or ♫

Spanish Tune

TWO OR MORE

Up till now the right hand fingers have always come to rest on the next string down. This is called a "top stroke". In this next section you will play two notes or more, at once. Instead of playing top strokes you will now have to take your finger or fingers away from the strings and not let them come to rest against the next ones.

The general rule is for:—

1. Single notes; play top strokes,

and for

2. Two or more notes; the thumb plays the lowest note and fingers play the top notes (not letting the fingers come to rest against the next string).

Sometimes there are exceptions to these two rules.

ALWAYS   push the string or strings slightly downwards as in the above diagram. This will give a large sound.

NEVER   pull the string or strings upwards as this will make the strings rattle against the frets.

MORE NOTES ON THE GUITAR

In future the figures in circles, (①,②,③, etc.) will indicate the string, Roman figures (I, II, III, etc.) will indicate the fret to use; figures not in circles (1 ,2, 3, etc.) will indicate the left hand finger to use.

The left hand fingering has been left out as from now on you might be asked to use any finger so as to fit in with the music.

Charles Gregory

A Sonatina

Joseph Kuffner

The Happy Clown

Whenever possible play top strokes for the top part. In bars 13 and 14 for the G chords, the thumb plays across all the strings from the bass to treble.

A Sonatina

Joseph Kuffner

Take notice of the right hand fingering.

Andante

Opus 246. F. Carulli

Study 8.

Use the fingering given for both hands. ♩♩♩ Play this triplet in the time of ♩♩

A Sonatina

Joseph Kuffner

When sliding the 1st and 2nd fingers (left hand) up the 2nd and 3rd strings from C and A to D and B be careful not to slur the notes. Try to slide the fingers as quickly as possible after leaving them on the notes for the full value. The D is on the 2nd string and the B is on the 3rd string.

CHORDS 1

ALWAYS   try to keep your fingers on the tips all the time.

NEVER   let your hand position be as above, as this will make your fingers touch other strings apart from the one you are supposed to be playing.

These chords are designed to give experience in accompanying at an early stage. They cannot give the same richness of sound produced by a full chord using all six strings.

Always keep the left hand fingers on the tips so that every note sounds. Memorize the chords as soon as possible.

The right hand thumb simply plays (or strums) across the 1st, 2nd and 3rd strings.

There are just two chords in the first part and they are:—

C major

G⁷ᵗʰ major

Skip to my Lou

Study 9.

Jimmy Crack Corn

Miss Molly

Having played the three string chords many times, try now the full chords.

C major

G⁷ᵗʰ major

CHORDS 2

In part 2 you will now have to use more than one left hand finger to play the chords. Try to place all the fingers used in the chord down on the strings at the same time, not one by one.

The chord fingerings are given before each piece of music.

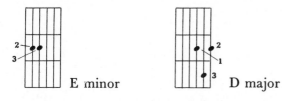

E minor   D major

What shall we do with a drunken sailor?

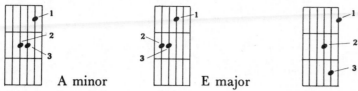

A minor   E major   D minor

Walking

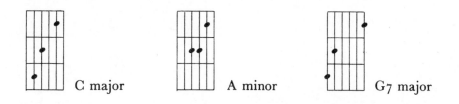

C major   A minor   G₇ major

Old MacDonald's Farm

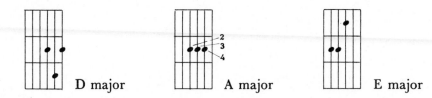

D major   A major   E major

Old French Folk Song

CHORDS 3

There are many chords using the "barree". The barree is the first left hand finger across some or all the strings with a chord fingering added.

Fig. 1

Fig. 2

In this diagram you can see the fingers are in the E major fingering but further up the strings. The barree has raised the chord from E up four semitones to G sharp. The chord is G sharp major. The secret of the barree is to keep the first finger as straight as possible and your left hand wrist well forward as in Fig. 1, not as in Fig. 2.

The "capotasto" is used frequently for changing the whole pitch of a song. Although good in some ways this device cannot be used when playing chords in different positions in quick succession, as it takes time to re-adjust.

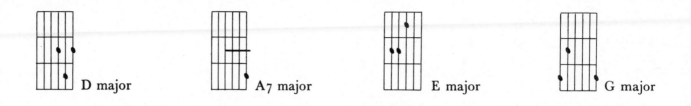

D major   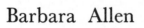A7 major   E major   G major

Barbara Allen

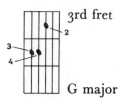

G major   C major

The other chords have been used before

The Reapers

François Couperin, 1668-1733
arranged C.G.

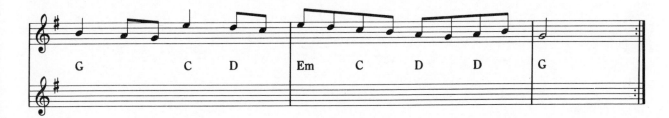

CHORD SYMBOLS

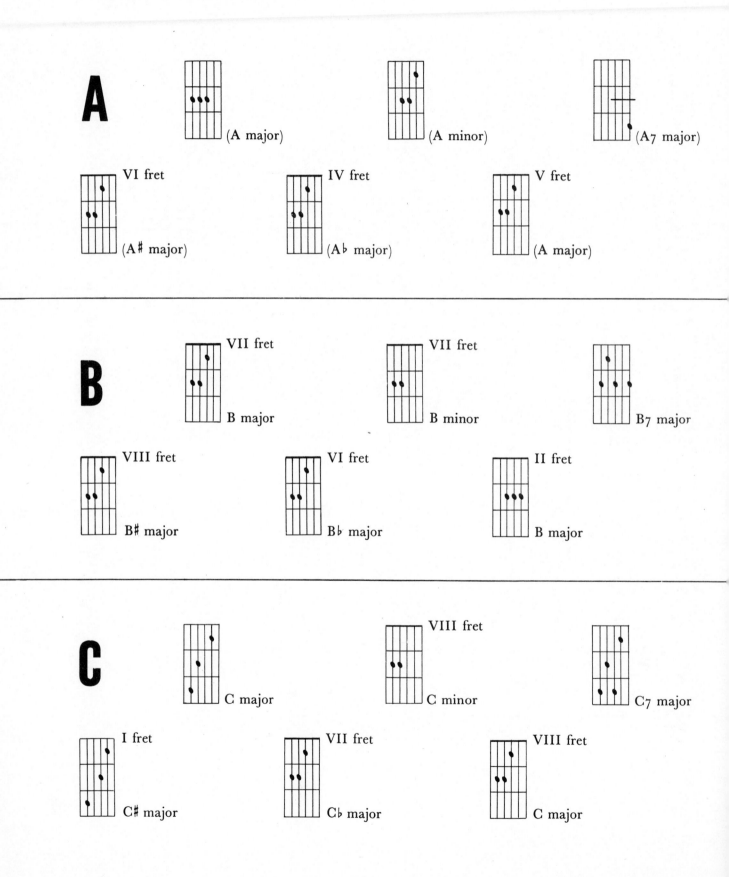

A

(A major)   (A minor)   (A7 major)

VI fret (A# major)   IV fret (Ab major)   V fret (A major)

B

VII fret B major   VII fret B minor   B7 major

VIII fret B# major   VI fret Bb major   II fret B major

C

C major   VIII fret C minor   C7 major

I fret C# major   VII fret Cb major   VIII fret C major

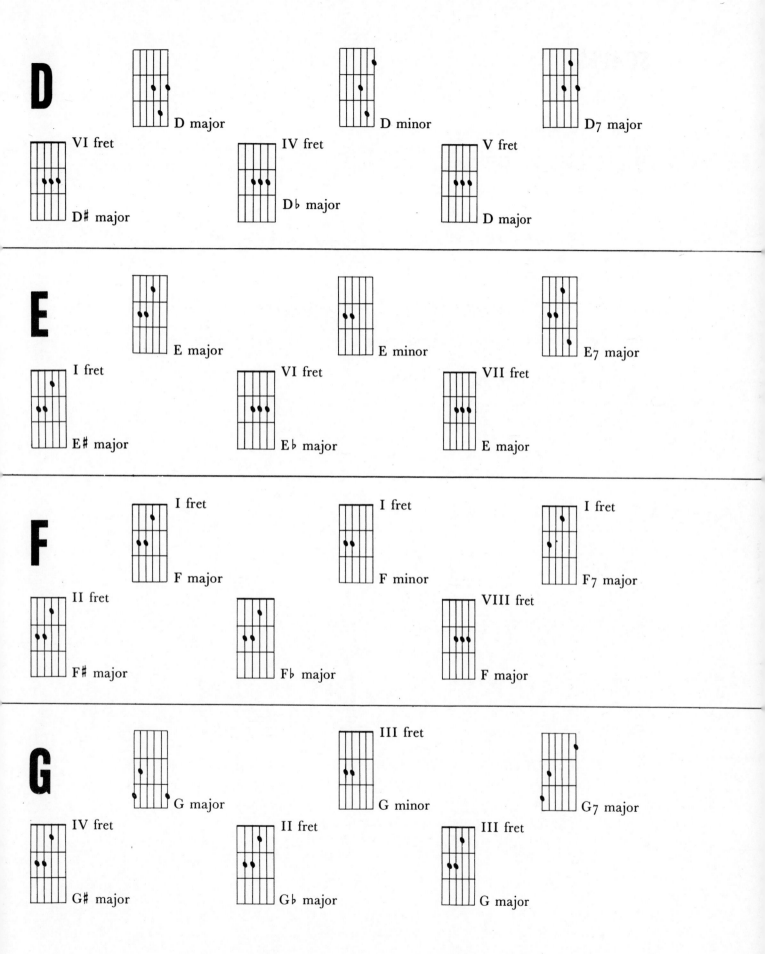

35

SCALES

C major

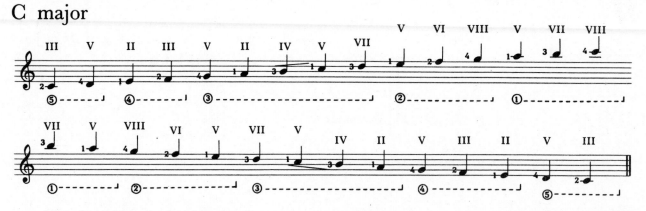

Play four times in the right hand (1, 2, 1, 2.) to each finger put down in the left hand. After some time play one note right hand to every left hand finger.

Other scales can be played by simply using the same fingering as above but starting on a different fret.

The scale of C major starts on the III fret.
„ „ „ C♯ „ „ „ „ IV „ .
„ „ „ D „ „ „ „ V „ .
„ „ „ D♯ „ „ „ „ VI „ .
„ „ „ E „ „ „ „ VII „ .

G major

The scale of G major starts on the III fret.
„ „ „ G♯ „ „ „ „ IV „ .
„ „ „ A „ „ „ „ V „ .
„ „ „ A♯ „ „ „ „ VI „ .
„ „ „ B „ „ „ „ VII „ .

C minor (harmonic)

The scale of C minor harmonic starts on the III fret.
   ,,   ,,   ,, C♯ ,,   ,,   ,, ,, ,, IV ,, .
   ,,   ,,   ,, D ,,   ,,   ,, ,, ,, V ,, .
   ,,   ,,   ,, D♯ ,,   ,,   ,, ,, ,, VI ,, .
   ,,   ,,   ,, E ,,   ,,   ,, ,, ,, VII ,, .

C minor (melodic)

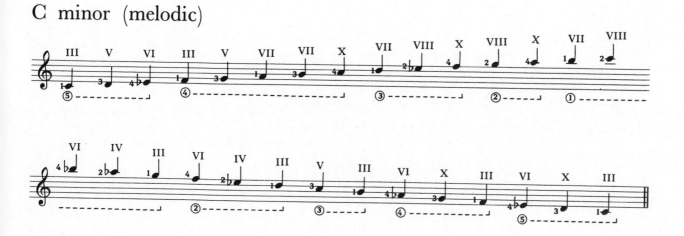

The scale of C minor melodic starts on the III fret.
   ,,   ,,   ,, C♯ ,,   ,,   ,, ,, ,, IV ,, .
   ,,   ,,   ,, D ,,   ,,   ,, ,, ,, V ,, .

RIGHT HAND EXERCISE

These exercises can at first be played on the open strings; after some practice a simple chord can then be added by the left hand.

Play on each string except the 6th string:—

(a) 1, 2, 1, 2.

(b) 2, 3, 2, 3.

(c) 1, 3, 1, 3.

(d) 1, 2, 3, 2.

For the next set of exercises keep a finger (right hand) for each string.

3rd finger on the 1st string.

2nd „ „ „ 2nd „

1st „ „ „ 3rd „

Thumb alternates on the bass strings.

(a) Th 1 2 3 2 1.

(b) Th 3 2 1 2 3.

(c) Th 1 2 1 3 1 2 1.

(d) Th 1 3 1 2 1 3 1.

(e) Th 2 1 2 3 2 1 2.

(f) Th 2 3 2 1 2 3 2.

(g) Th 3 1 3 2 3 1 3.

(h) Th 3 2 3 1 3 2 3.

ALWAYS let each finger come to rest against the string which is after the string you have just played.